Numbers

EVERYWHERE

by **LINDA LEOPOLD STRAUSS**

Illustrated by
SARA INFANTE

YAY!

HOLIDAY HOUSE · NEW YORK

For my family, who helped me find numbers everywhere!
—L.L.S.

To Mom and Dad—faithful
cheerleaders and tireless team.
I see your love for us everywhere.
—S.I.

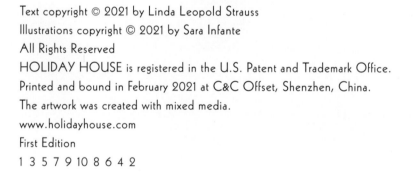

Text copyright © 2021 by Linda Leopold Strauss
Illustrations copyright © 2021 by Sara Infante
All Rights Reserved
HOLIDAY HOUSE is registered in the U.S. Patent and Trademark Office.
Printed and bound in February 2021 at C&C Offset, Shenzhen, China.
The artwork was created with mixed media.
www.holidayhouse.com
First Edition
1 3 5 7 9 10 8 6 4 2

Library of Congress Cataloging-in-Publication Data

Names: Strauss, Linda Leopold, author. | Infante, Sara, illustrator.
Title: Numbers everywhere / Linda Leopold Strauss ; illustrated by Sara Infante.
Description: First edition. | New York : Holiday House, 2021. | Audience: Ages 3–6 |
Audience: Grades K–1 | Summary: "Fun rhymes and pictures help children with number
recognition and identification"—Provided by publisher.
Identifiers: LCCN 2020036262 | ISBN 9780823443215 (hardcover)
Subjects: LCSH: Counting—Juvenile literature. | Numbers in art—Juvenile literature.
Classification: LCC QA113 .S86 2021 | DDC 513.2/11—dc23
LC record available at https://lccn.loc.gov/2020036262

ISBN: 978-0-8234-4321-5 (hardcover)

Look up, look down,

Look here, look there.

Number shapes are

Everywhere.

0

A zero is round

Like a sparkly ring.

There's nothing inside it—

Not one single thing.

Start with zero—counting's fun! Turn the page for number one....

A tall straight line

Is number one,

A rocket headed

Toward the sun!

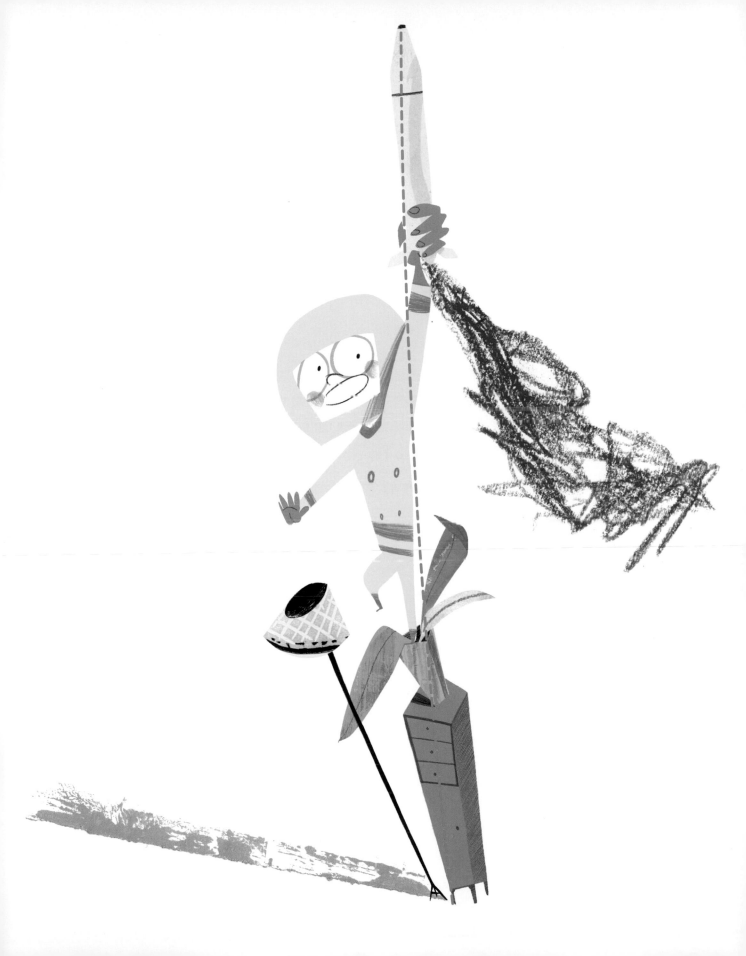

With a curve round and down,

And a flat line below—

Two's a swan on a pond

Where the marsh grasses grow.

Curve out and back in—
Do it once, then repeat:
A three is red pepper
On pizza. Let's eat!

4

A triangle balanced
On top of a line—
Four's a sail on the sea
On a day that is fine.

5

Five's flat, and then down,

Then a curve on one side

Like a shiny red tricycle—

Hop on and ride!

A loop and a curve

From its head to its tail:

Add flippers to six

And it looks like a whale!

A seven is two lines,

One sideways, one down—

Like the street lights that light up

The night in your town.

An eight is two circles,

One high and one low—

Like the jolly fat fellow

You build out of snow.

YAY!

Nine starts with a circle,

Then curves down and back,

Like a half-eaten pretzel

Left over from snack.

Down and up and here and there,

Number shapes are everywhere.

So turn the page and have a try. . . .

How many numbers can you spy?

0

1

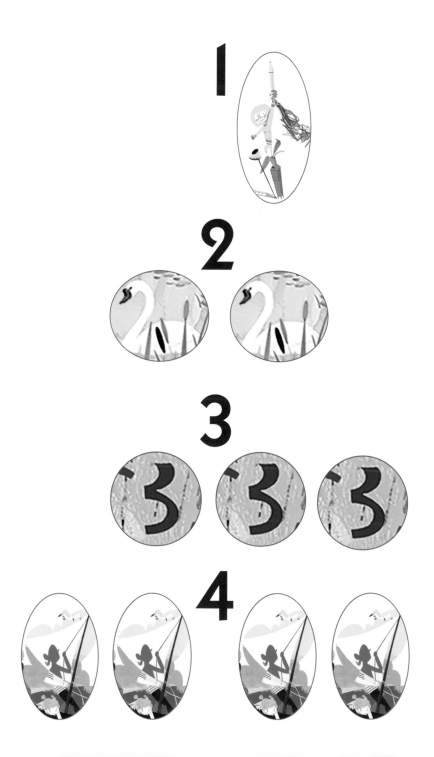

2

3

4